Jacob's Ladder

Genesis 28:10–22 for Children
Written by Virginia Mueller
Illustrated by Michelle Dorenkamp

ARCH® Books
Copyright © 1990
Concordia Publishing House
3558 S. Jefferson Avenue, St. Louis, MO 63118-3968
Manufactured in the United States of America

Poor Jacob was in trouble.
He had to leave his home.
His twin named Esau hated him.
He had to go alone.

His father, Isaac, blessed him
And said, "Now listen, son,
It's time for you to find a wife.
The Lord will give you one."

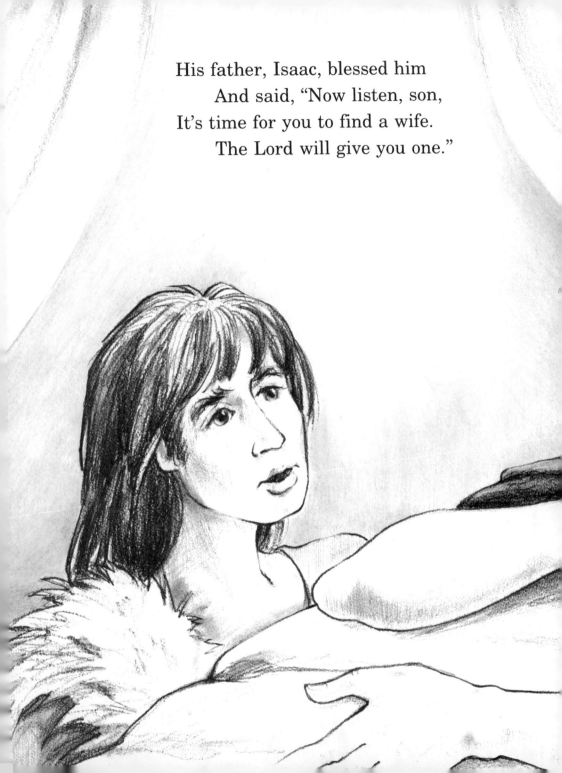

Sad Jacob started on his trip,
Afraid to face his brother.
He worried as he left his home,
His father, and his mother.

He didn't have attendants
    Or a camel caravan.
He walked away with staff in hand,
    A sad and lonely man.

He walked along the lonesome road
    Four hundred miles away.
And as the sun was setting,
    He found a place to stay.

He didn't have a sleeping bag
    Or warm and comfy bed.
He didn't have a pillow
    To rest his weary head.

Instead, he slept upon the ground;
    His head upon a stone!
Poor Jacob tossed and turned that night.
    He thought he was alone.

As Jacob slept, he dreamed he saw
    A ladder—very high!
A shining, stretching stairway
    That reached from earth to sky.

Bright angels traveled up and down.
    On top, stood God in glory.
And Jacob heard God talk to him
    And tell this wondrous story.

"I am the God of Abraham
And God of Isaac, too.
This land on which you lie tonight
Was meant to pass to you.

"Your children shall be as the dust,
    Spread north, south, east, and west.
And through you and your children
    All people will be blest.

        "I'll keep My promises to you.
          I'll guard you everywhere.
        And I will never leave you,
          As you are in My care."

The vision of the ladder
     Put fear in Jacob's heart.
He suddenly awakened
     And sat up with a start!

"This place is heaven's gate!" he cried.
　　"I heard God's voice speak here.
But surely it's the house of God,
　　So I don't need to fear."

At daylight Jacob took his stone
    And stood it straight and tall.
He named his resting place God's house,
    For he had heard God's call.

Now Jacob was not worried.
    He knew God blessed his life.
He'd make up with his brother
    And find a loving wife.

When you are sad and worried
And feel you're all alone,
Just think of Jacob's pillow,
That hard and lumpy stone!

There is no night too dark for God.
He sees you everywhere.
Just trust in Him to light your way
And keep you in His care.

Dear Parents,

You may want to read the background for this story in Gen. 27–28:9, in which Jacob steals his brother Esau's birthright. Esau threatens to kill him, and their mother Rebekah advises Jacob to run and hide at the home of his Uncle Laban in Haran. His father, Isaac, adds the command to find a suitable wife among his own relatives. To simplify the story for your child, explain that Jacob is worried because he has had a fight with his brother, he must find a wife, and he must travel alone to an unknown land. Focus on the worry Jacob feels because he is depending on himself rather than trusting in God's care.

Although this story is popularly titled *Jacob's Ladder*, Jacob actually saw something resembling a stairway or sloping steps in his dream. Jacob looked into heaven and saw almighty God and the angels who perfectly obey His will. Jacob realized how foolish he had been to depend on himself. Even though he had lied, cheated, and stolen, God still loved him. Assure your child that no night is too dark, no trouble too severe, that God will not be there.

Stones were often used in the Old Testament to mark special events (Gen. 31:45–54; Ex. 24:4; Joshua 4:1–9; 1 Sam. 7:12). Abraham had first pitched his tent at Bethel (meaning "house of God") and now Jacob realized God's presence there and trusted Him to keep him in His care.

Jesus is our stairway between heaven and earth. He gave His life to bridge the gap created by sin and bring us close to God.

The Editor